SPACE TRIP

SPACE TRIP

Carol Louise Guest

Todd & Honeywell, Inc.
Great Neck, New York / 1981

First Edition

Published by Todd & Honeywell, Inc.
Ten Cuttermill Road
Great Neck, New York 11021

ISBN 0-89962-047-7

Manufactured in the United States of America

Contents

Dedicated to Harold Stahl, Dan La Verdiere, and Nancy McEvoy, without whose support and inspiration this book would never have been possible.

ABORTION

I had an abortion today
It wasn't the usual kind
For it wasn't of the body
It was of the mind

I ripped out all the pieces
Of the love I had for you
I killed the word "forever"
Hope and love are through

I wandered through the forest of my soul
And wondered in amazement
What I saw in you, that made me lose complete control

The strange part is that I feel sorrier for you than me
For you lost the best of my love that now could never be.

FRAGILITY

Like a doctor who performs a delicate heart operation
Who scrubs up and puts on his surgical gloves
You must prepare to be tender with my heart
You must hold it as you would a stained glass window
Admire its virtues
Fondle it with "I love you's"
But do not drop it in haste or carelessness
For then you would shatter the very essence of my soul
Into infinite nothingness
Do not stifle or mutilate
For irreparable damage could occur
This heart will self-destruct under pressure,
Like an aspirin in water.

NATURAL DISASTERS

The Titanic went down
The 747 crashed in mid-air
The volcano erupted
But I wasn't there
The earthquake hit Mexico
The floods came everywhere
The ice storm hit us suddenly
But still I didn't care
Until you said "NEVER"
And that cut like a knife
But your eyes were filled with tears
And they said other things

DISARMED

You caught me in mid-air
And my heart in my hand
It was love growing here
But nothing I had planned
You're only about 360 degrees from what I had planned you to be
They say that love is blind-
Now I think I see
Our verbal vibrations are always right on
So why can't we get it together?
We're constantly reaching out
So why aren't we touching each other?
The winter snow is only tolerated
Because we know that spring is not far away
So I can only struggle through life
Because you're here in my heart to stay.

INTANGIBLE

I love you, as long as the constant rain
As warm as an August night
As soft as a kitten's purr
As long as the stars are bright
Without hesitation,
And no reservation
You bring out the most of the best in me.
You light up my life,
You negate all my strife
You really shake my tree!
The cars and the furs,
The clothes and the shoes
They don't mean a thing
If I could have you, above all these
Then my heart should sing.

CAN OF WORMS

When you offered me no promises,
No rainbows or seeds of hope,
I would have chosen to be a mindless moron,
A freak of nature upon whom people stare with scorn and ridicule,
An aborted fetus who never knew life,
An illiterate pagan who never heard the four-letter word "love",
A dead dog with his guts all over the street
Anything but what I was-
Alive and breathing,
Seething and scorched by my love for you.

PARADOX

I am soft
You are loud
You're for real
I'm a cloud
You smile,
And I'm proud
To relate.

ROMANCE

In this world of booming progress
I think it's time to regress
And ban the boom
And make some room for Romance.
If we dare to be so bold
As to block out mass confusion
While we conjure up illusion
Of the soul
I'm tired of waiting
And computer dating
And escalating the war
and not the love
And words that chase at meaning
In a shallow hopeless way
And the promise of tomorrow
We cannot find today.
And the stifling heat of Realism
That smothers all my dreams
And the frigid frost of reason
That obliterates my schemes.
For it's really elementary
Like a hand fits in a glove
One and one makes two
And two make love
And that's enough.

WHERE ANGELS FEAR TO TREAD

Like the wind on the turbulent sea
Your presence evokes a desire in me
To stir up the inner sanctum
Of your creative psyche,
Endlessly.

WHAT WILL BECOME OF ME?

What will become of me?
What will become of me, my love?
Like the bird that cannot sing
The watch that cannot run
Without you, I'm lost.
Like the compass that doesn't know the direction
Or the little girl that wants protection
That's what I am.
Awaiting the day in which I can mingle and shine in your life
Like a little star that's set on fire
Like a little star that's set on fire
That finally reaches completion
In the broader sky of another
That now knows true fulfillment.

TWO DIFFERENT WORLDS

Holding your head back in a swing
Letting your heart take wings
Building castles in the sand
Holding a baby robin in your hand
Walking sedately through the park
Whistling a song, like a lark
Seeing a circus or a baby kitten, for the first time
The last lick of your favorite sucker, lemon or lime
Giving your heart away on impulse
To some beautiful person you don't even know
Holding hands through life
And watching your love grow
Creating together one unique human being
Creating together your own private work of art,
That never before has been
And the whole cycle repeats itself again.

UNSTABLE AS EVER

Love is gay, love is frustrating
Just when you think you're in the rating
You find out you're not
And then you silently rot
And decay and slither away
And what does he care?
And then he smiles
And you're up in the air
How can I break this crazy spell
This crazy hot fever
And cease to think of him,
Or his name forever?

VALUES

I chanced to meet some people on the road of life
They told me of their gladness and their strife
If you will listen now and listen well
Heed the words I say, the tale I tell
The first man had great silver and much gold
He invested well; he bought and sold
The more his money multiplied, the more he swelled with pride
Till one day Death came knocking at his door
And he cried, "Wait, I need time to make more"
Alas, his cry, too late in vain,
His beloved treasure was his bane
Another man I saw had great antiques,
Of every shape and size
Which required great protection, as you would surmise
One hapless day a robber took them all away
Now, the man beside himself, wonders who will repay.
Now I see a lady friend of great beauty and dress
She wants to be in the limelight, the symbol of success
But as she walks by a mirror, she sees a wrinkle in her face
Oh, hideous shame and disgrace
For more shall there appear, then what shall she do?
She cannot make her face anew
And that's her whole life
The last man I met had neither great wealth or fame
What he did have was a virtuous name
He said, "Material things cannot follow in death",
"Neither can we stay the hand of time"
"No respecter of persons is death"
"We don't always see the reason or the rhyme".

But even in death
A good name lives on
People do remember
Can virtue live forever?

DICK AND JANE REVISITED

Look, look
See Dick
Dick is Macho
See Jane
Jane is Foxy
Dick and Jane Live Together In A Condominium
Full Of Pandemonium
Dick and Jane Think Free Love Is Where It's At
They Both Do Their Own Thing
Who Needs A Crummy Piece Of Paper And A Ring?
They Have Zero Dependents Because Babies Cramp Their Style
They Have Total Liberation
So Why Do They Never Smile?

DICHOTOMY

Prices are high, morals are low
Alice is a man
Kiss is a group
Men walk on the moon
And women walk on men
People smoke "pot" and "grass", cigarettes are a "drag"
Speed is a hyper
And life is a downer
"Gay" is frustrating
And being "straight" is aggravating
Being "straight" is square and honesty doesn't have a prayer
To "get yourself together" you must tear yourself apart
Scrutinize your motives
And make a new start
We're turned on like gas
We're turned off like a light
Where is our guru to tell us what's right?
Each person racing in the Indy 500 of his life
What if we forgot where we're going?

THE URGENCY OF NOW

I wanted to say "I love You", but it was too late
The autumn day was too warm and the job was too important
And I was too young
I saw you looking better and the doctor said O.K.
He'll be home next week
And I kissed you on the forehead
But I didn't know that was the last kiss
And people were yelling and screaming
Because the Tigers were tasting sublime victory after
a long sweaty struggle
And all the noise was like jaded hypocrisy
And all I knew was a vacuum of darkness inside my guts

BLOODY MURDER

I Love You! I Do! I Promise Forever!
I *Love* You
I Love *You*
We
Us
Mr. & Mrs.
Mr. & Mrs. & Baby
Mr. & Mrs. & Family
Us (Collective Unit)
We Love Everyone, Each Other
Shared Response, Love And No Pretense
I Don't Love *You*
I Don't Love *Them*
I Don't *Love*
I *Don't*
I! I! I!
Gross Rip-Off
Don't Deplore The Snake On His Belly,
He's Looking Down On You

MOTHER

M is for the many things you taught us
O is for the open love you gave
T is for the tenderness you brought us
H is for the happy home we have
E is for every day you helped us
R is for respect we have for you inside

Put them all together,
They spell Mother
A Six Letter Word For Love, Personified

INSTANT REPLAY

I remember my waiting in the car
And soft pajamas that felt good and smelled good
And going to pick you up after work
And going to get hamburgers
They were better than a steak dinner
My eyes would scan the sea of faces
Until I saw your face
And I would think "There's my Daddy - he's the best"
You always brought me a little treat
A coconut candy bar
But I can't find those candy bars anymore
And you are gone
And I miss my little treat
But I miss you more
The memories are like old movies
They stay in my head
And console me on sad days.

FRIEND

I call you friend
You are greater than wealth or fame
For when these have deserted me
You still know my name
I come to you in times of trouble
You help relieve my grief
I come to you in times of joy
And find a sweet relief
I share my tears and laughs with you
With you I bare my soul
When I feel half a person
You help to make me whole
So be there when I need you
And listen when I'm blue
If you should turn your back on me
Who knows what I'd do?

ODE TO A RIGHT ON BROTHER (DAVID B. GUEST)

Brother, there's no other quite like you
A sweller feller can't be found
From here to Timbuktu
You're always there to lend a helping hand
As Mr. Fix-It, I think you're just grand
Like just the other day, my tire went flat
And I really didn't know where I was at
You knew just what to do and how to do it
And I just stood around and said "I blew it"
To mention all your virtues here
I'd run out of time and space
So let me just say this
As a brother you take 1st place!

FUTILITY

Tears of fickle, fancy days
On concrete walls of business as usual
Occasionally infiltrating
By momentary verbal massages
Read in-between the lines
Empty deception
Frugal force without impact
Pretty, passive, putrefying words
Of consoling, colossal friends.

Emotional illiterate
Fool of a beggar
Waiting for a hand-out
Fingers of freedom and fantasy turned into ice
Words without feeling
Lost from their context
Run with feeling, till it stops and hits you in the face
How can love and hate live side by side?
Be almost one?
A volcano building
Hot lava burning the insides out
A false maturity
Distortions, diversions, derision, decisions
Little me with big ideals
Vultures of truth
Descending on my ideals
Nurtured by self-desire
Torn masks
Nothing is real
But what I feel for today.
Steal away on silent steps of self-pity
Don't turn back
You've made your point
Who could understand?
Christen me confusion
Should have known better
Thanks for the memories.

MUSIC, MASTER OF MY SOUL

Oh, music master of my soul
Renaissance anew
What subtle beauty thou revealest
What immortal, lustrous hue
Music, thou speakest with more eloquent tongue
What precious words of thee are sung
Thou dost surpass all human limitations
To unforseen hopes and unborn expectations
Thou holdest me in silent captivation
By thy lulling notes so tender
As they fall on ever eager ears
To my being, joy they render
Let me view your hidden treasures
And survey your vast domain
For long after mortal man has faded
Immortal music, thou dost remain
Music keen and bright
By thee my soul is led
For thou dost traverse to peaks unknown
Where others fear to tread
Music that can create any mood I choose
And make my soul rush to and fro
Or slumber with peaceful, quiet visions
This music I must better know
Music, like a subtle stranger
Thou canst come and quickly flee
But dear subtle stranger
What impact you leave on me

Thou canst cast out woes and fears
Kindle happiness and dry my tears
Thou, immortal healer of my soul
Thou, alone, canst make me whole
Music, let me rest on thine outspread wings
And dream of future hopes and better things
Things that some would dare not see
Music, I find these in thee

GENTLEMAN JIM

He's my Southern Comfort on the telephone line each day
He makes me laugh and smile
He can chase the blues away
He knows just the right word
To ease the stress and strain
Just to hear his voice
Is a glad refrain
So if you're down and out, and need a real friend
Just give him a call
He's a Super Scorpio to the end!

Dedicated to Jim Hughes—GMAD Doraville

IF I COULD

If I could choose the life
I think would suit me best
I'd choose the simple one
Of peace and joy and rest
I'd live alone
like Henry Thoreau
Enjoy my life
I want you to know!
Each day some jewel I would find
Some morsel of hope to nourish my mind
And I would feast on these
And they would be my sustenance
Like the air we breathe.
My music, books, and thoughts
I would carry there with me
I'd study in each one of them
How happy I would be!
I'd observe the wondrous nature
The beauty here on earth
Then I'd let my soul run over
With peace, and joy, and mirth.
Each day I'd give thanks
To the Dear One above
Who made this great earth
In kindness and love
And made a beautiful garden for man to live in
But foolish man lost it because of his sin.
Then I'd watch the rushing world
As it quickly passed me by
With all its finite pleasures
And then I'd ask, Why?
Why does the world go on like this?
Rushing to who knows where
For what's there to face but destruction?

But then, who really cares?
But, alas, I wake from this perfect world
Where I am content all alone
And find myself bound by the fetters of life
And then I begin to groan!
Then I wish that Thoreau
might live again today
And remind us how to live again
In his simple, rewarding way!

DAY AND NIGHT

Watch Day as she awakes
As her sleepy head she shakes
And throws a misty haze
O'er all her inhabitants
And sheer beauty to each viewer grants!
Watch her,
As each sleeping child she wakes,
And each his course blissfully takes!
Day is like our life
So short and brief
Full of inspiration,
Sadness and grief.
So catch each moment
As Time pulls it away
Do what you would do
And say what you would say
Delve into knowledge, see her soul
Treasure her jewels precious and rare
Tell others you love them
And show them you care.
Sing when trials are near
And in days of war and fear
Look up to God above
And all around at manifestations of His love!
Exercise your body and your soul
Plan your future, set your goal
Grasp faith to help surpass the trials ever near
And hope to overshadow all your fear.

TO EACH HIS OWN

To each his own ecstacy
In whatever form it may be.
To a baby
A gentle caress
Makes a blanket of happiness.
A warm bottle, encased within a mother's love
A soft diaper, a cozy bed, he's dreaming of
However small of insignificant as the breeze
A baby you may please with these.
For a toddler its a yearning to explore
To discover what your hands are for
Open up the cupboard door
And bring out pots and pans galore.
To a little darling
It's a dimpled doll
Whose worth is beyond measure
For simply dressing and feeding her
Brings her infinite maternal pleasure.
To junior its a jaunt in fields afar
Where he can gather fireflies,
And house them in a jar
Or alleys with garbage cans abundant with goods
Silverware, saving stamps, magazines, and wood.
To a teenager, it's the urge to dress like all her friends
To write in diaries
Or talk on the telephone without end.
A first job
A first car
These are major milestones by far
To a collegian
Its ivy league and lots of books
Sorority, fraternity, and terribly good looks
An attractive honor point average
And not feeling like a "snook".

To a woman
It's the unspoken word
The mutual glance
Of inner joy
The feeling that your unconquerable hero is just a little boy.
To lovers its a walk in the park
A kiss in the dark.
To a bride,
It's a feeling deep inside
Of feminine pride
That she is the most beautiful and fortunate
woman on earth
A handsome groom at her side
A love that will always abide
Despite a wordly tide
Of gossip, hate, and maliciousness
These are her happiness.
To me, it's sticking my toes in a stream
Or dreaming the impossible dream.
To grandma and grandpa, it's sharing aches or pains
Or the joyous refrain of a baby babbling in their outstretched arms
Stealing hearts with awesome baby charms.
It's growing old in peace with God and man
Knowing we've accomplished all we can.

DAY IN SIGHT

Oh day eternal, fast approaching
How we long to see your face
When we can say with pride and honor
We have finished half the race.
We have plodded and been prodded twelve long years
Up education's mountain
We long to reach the top at last
And drink of freedom's fountain.
And now you've caught us unawares
We're glad but we're afraid
Of future years and future tears
Commitments to be made.
Like a fading shadow
Our high school years pass by
How the memories linger
But how the moments fly!
We've finished half the race
But the coming half holds more to fear
For life demands our constant action
A valiant soul in a world so drear.
So let us now with dedication
Push ever upward to the crest
That we might say with God's great help
"We've reached the top, we've done our best".

Class Poem
June 1966

GLITTER GONE

Snowflakes glitter on, like little sparkles of my dreams
But yet it seems,
Your sparkles fade away
Like bubbles, into cold and gray
Reality.
And what is, is not
But for a dreamer's half-born thought
Death and birth, the self-same moment-nought.

SILENT SPLENDOR

I'm living in a cut-glass fairyland
Where trees weep, laden with the weight of icy tears
And baby snowflakes gleam and wink at me
For His magnificence is here, in all I see.
Traffic lights wear funny, icy chins
Some have even lost their colored grins
Untainted nature makes a new debut
And makes me know,
That it shall live for all eternity
By reason of one virtue: awesome simplicity
With this, my soul leaps up in ecstacy
And I say, "Nature, live on, for I live on in Thee".

THE FISH

The fish that wants to swim
Free in the stream of life
That wants to wander
Through new rivers
I am a sensitive fish
But there are two fish that live in me
And the two always want to fight
One lives on the earth
The other in the sea
That is why I cannot exist
Completely in harmony with myself.

YOUTH, FOREVER FREE

Oh, little ones
Who wave your flags so free
If you could only realize why it is
Why it must be

That many die across the sea for you
That freedom might prevail
And freedom true

That the blood of many
Still today seeps out on foreign soil
As your free land staggers beneath
The chains of sin
And wails the chant of turmoil

And men would vainly say that God is dead
While they weep and shudder
Circled in by their own dread
Shackled by their own desire
Sinking deeper in their self-made quagmire

Little ones, look and then beware
Lest you yourselves fall into the same snare
While you are young and free
Listen to the voice of God
That yours a better land may be
A peaceful land, where happiness has trod.

OBLIGATIONS

For better or for worse
I know not which it be
There's no one in the world who's quite like me
Who feeds on dreams
And thrives on fantasy.

In love, the fetters of my soul are broken
By some subtle smile or gem that's spoken
And my soul cannot contain
Nor e'er restrain
That simple joy

Immense thorn of maturity
Forever pricking at my soul to see
What I, delighting in its fancies good
Would begin to be

I cannot yet this thorn obliterate
Can I a mortal read the mind of Fate?
Or know what He has planned that I should be
This frail mortal of absurdity?

WHAT WILL I BECOME?

I am one person
That lives and yet at the same time
I am molded by every person I know
Happy, lively, and sad sentiments.
I live to serve others
And I am everyone
Because inside of my heart lives a part of everyone of you.

OMNIPRESENT UNCERTAINTY

Tottering on the legs of adolescence
Groping at unattainable adulthood
Seizing tenaciously for illusory love
Haunted by complexity
Deafened by monotony
Nauseated by superiority
Befuddled by diversity
Grappling at nothing

SIGHTSEEING

Crucifixion is the silent mourner in the corner
Hollow heart with repercussions of internal hemorrhaging
Sandpaper implications that singe and slice
And sacrifice all of life's hopes and values
On the brazen altar of status.

The ostentatious oligarchy that parades across your psyche.
Like pre-cut paper dolls, complete with all the trimmings

Hang out your emotions to drip-dry
Virtue and honesty self-destruct
Nothing talks faster than a buck
Catch a glimpse of the bland white sepulchre of your soul
What a tragic thought
You were half, but now you're naught.

SPACES

Train and track
Can't go back
Strain and black
And doors that separate one from another

Drawn faces
Warm embraces
And empty places - inside and out

A big pine box slides down from the train
A misty rain is falling
And a surging pain is reaching to the sinews of your soul

A numbing grief
Then some relief
For He is there
In the words of a prayer
His presence near will calm each fear.

IMAGES OF LIFE

TIGHT
LOOSE
FREE
CRY
MILK
SLEEP
SEE
GROW
TO KNOW
FORM
SHAPE
COLOR
MEANING
SEARCH
FIND
PLAY
DREAM
TAKE
TALK
SHARE

FACE
CONFLICT
SMALL
ODDBALL
TOO MUCH
WANT
CAN'T HAVE
HESITATE
FRUSTRATE
IRATE
TOO LATE
GREAT!
WINK
SMILE
WORD
GROOVE
COMMUNICATE
MUTUAL
BEE TOUCHES
INSIDE OF
FLOWER
SUCKS HONEY

IRRITATION
ADMIRATION
EXCITATION
STIMULUS
RESPONSE
PERPETUAL
CONFIRMATION
ASSURANCE
ASSENT
"I DO"
PEOPLE
STAND
CARE
CRY
SMILE
THANK YOU
BYE
RICE
SHOES
NEW ENVIRON-
MENT
SEX

TO DO THINGS
DIFFERENT
DOUBLE BLISS
TROUBLE
EXPAND
EXPENSE
OUT OF SELF
UP TIGHT
OUT OF SIGHT
FEELING BLUE
YOU
THE ORIGINA-
TOR
MATURE
ACCEPT
PERPETUATE
GLOW
GROW
LOOSE
FREE
CRY
OH, MY CHILD!
GIFTS

RIFTS
TIME
TWO
DEPEND
INSEPARABLE
TWO CHECKS
PAINS
DEFECTS
OFFEND
PRETEND
HURT
EGO
BIFOCALS

CORNS
FORLORN
FACT
FACE
OVER WITH
QUICK
SIGH
DIE
NO SOUND
BUT THE
GROUND
OVER ME
AROUND ME.

"BEING THERE"

In this maniacal and sometimes masochistic existence
I thank God for small treasures like you
Your listening eyes and feeling heart and kindred spirit
Soothe my troubled psyche
Like water on a burn
Our good vibrations are nurtured and supported
By mutual caring-ness
So our friendship accrues interest and matures
And becomes better and better
Until a powerful new force is born, and revived,
And becomes again and again like a pleasant breeze in the desert.

P.S. May the Force of friendship
be with you always!